Also by Elizabeth N. Doyd

Write Him Off: 30 Days to Healing Your Broken Heart

The Love Book: Writing Your Way to Your Soul Mate

The Science of Getting Rich Action Plan: Decoding Wallace D. Wattles's Bestselling Book

7 Days to Minimalistic Living: A Stress-Free Guide to Declutter, Clean and Organize Your Home and Your Life

GRATITUDE JOURNAL

52 Writing Prompts to Celebrate Your Wonderful Life

Elizabeth N. Doyd

ISBN-13: 978-1987859027

ISBN-10: 1987859022

Contents

How to Use This Book   7

GRATITUDE JOURNAL PROMPTS   13
1: The Best Day of Your Life   15
2: All Smiles   17
3: Teacher's Pet   19
4: The Sixth Sense   21
5: The Bright Side   23
6: Our Other Mother   25
7: Cinema Paradisco   27
8: Kids Say the Darndest Things   29
9: Just Desserts   31
10: The Magic Mirror   33
11: Regarde Le Ciel   35
12: A Night at the Museum   37
13: Family Matters   39
14: Bookworm   43
15: A Tale of One City   45
16: The Shirt Off My Back   47
17: Your Gifts   49
18: Art Attack   51
19: A Season of Fate's Perfection   53
20: Good to Great   55
21: Happy Meals   57
22: Travel Bug   59
23: All You Need is Love   61
24: The Adventures of...   63
25: I Feel Good   65

26: God is My DJ   67
27: Happy Birthday   69
28: Where the Heart Is   71
29: Best Gift Ever   73
30: Role Models   75
31: Funny Face   77
32: Hope Floats   79
33: A Little Help From Our Friends   81
34: The Art of Doing Nothing   83
35: Please Give   85
36: Please Take   87
37: DIY   89
38: The Way You Move Me   91
39: Momento   93
40: The Transporter   95
41: The Grand Palace   97
42: It's in the Photograph   99
43: Animal Farm   101
44: Home Run   103
45: The Work   105
46: The Best Time of the Year   107
47: The Patriot   109
48: Flattery Will Get You Everywhere   111
49: Money in My Pocket   113
50: Straight Fs   115
51: Mere Mortals   117
52: Never Stop Learning   119
More Ideas   121

About the Author   125

How to Use This Book

Writing in a gratitude journal will only take a few minutes of your day, but doing so has the power to turn your entire life around.

When we start counting the little things that we treasure, things that may otherwise escape our attention in the chaos of daily life, we are making the effort to be more positive, and thus more loving, giving and appreciative people.

Our happiness is nobody's responsibility but our own; when we make the effort to stop reacting to the people and circumstances around us, we're taking back control of our lives in order to steer it in the direction we want to go.

Giving thanks to the universe is giving love, and what we give inevitably comes back to us. Once you make a habit out of appreciating all the gifts in life, big or small, you'll begin attracting more positive people and situations. Bad habits and former worries will disappear, replaced by faith and good feeling toward yourself and others.

Think about gratitude in terms of food. While complaining about life and reaching for your third donut of the day may give you a temporary hit of energy, both will inevitably send you crashing in the short term, and be detrimental to your health in the long term.

Conversely, feeling love and gratitude is akin to choosing to consume pure, wholesome foods full of vitamins and minerals, such as fresh vegetables and whole grains. Not only will your body, mind and soul be properly nourished, you are contributing to lifelong health.

One of the most powerful laws of the universe, the Law of Attraction, says that whatever you focus on grows stronger. By making a habit to focus on the positive side of things, even something you might label as negative, you are tapping into the secret of living a happy life.

Starting a gratitude journal is easy. All you need is a pen, a notebook, and a moment to lay down your appreciation for what you've been given in life.

Here are some ways you can begin each entry:

Thank you…

I'm thankful for…

Today is wonderful because…

I'm proud of myself for…

I'm so grateful for…

Counting my blessings in…

What a welcome surprise that…

I love…

I appreciate…

I'm blessed with…

This book contains journal prompts on 52 different topics. You can focus on one topic a week if you wish—that's enough to last you a year. Or you may pick and choose a prompt at random if you are looking for inspiration and new ideas on any given day.

Most people begin a gratitude journal by listing the basic things they have, necessities such as a roof over their heads, loving family members, supportive friends, a healthy body, and food and water to keep them alive. No matter what, these are always things to be grateful for. Many people in the world are not blessed with such luxuries.

Daily Ritual

Writing in your gratitude journal for at least 21 days straight will help make it a habit. It's a great habit to form, but be careful not to overdo it. If you're struggling and forcing yourself to find five or ten new things to be grateful for every day, it might be counterproductive if you are stressing yourself out if they are not coming easily to you.

One to three new entries are doable. It may even be more beneficial to read over your older entries. The point is that writing in this journal should be a fun, happy experience. Be flexible with yourself. Write at the time when you're most comfortable, at a pace that you prefer.

If you find yourself repeating items, it helps to get more specific.

For example, if you are grateful for your loving husband, instead of writing "Thank you for my loving husband", you can go into detail as to why:

"I appreciate that John listened to my story and laughed at my jokes today."

"I love John for giving me a warm hug this morning before going to work."

"I'm so grateful that John took the time to call me when he's busy at the office."

If you love yoga class, instead of writing, *"I love doing yoga",* how about:

"I'm so grateful that my yoga instructor showed us a new pose today."

"I love the harmonious energy of everyone in my yoga class."

"Today, I'm proud that I can go deeper in this yoga pose."

Weekly Ritual

If your life is hectic, writing in the journal once or twice a week may be enough for you. If you think of writing in your journal every day as a chore, another thing to complete on your to-do list, it won't produce the good feelings that you're aiming for. If you can write more, great, but writing more doesn't always equal being more grateful. Simply leafing through the journal and perusing some old entries might just get you in a happier state all the quicker.

My goal for you is that your journal will lift your spirits when you read back on your own entries. Let's get started.

— Elizabeth N. Doyd

Gratitude Journal

Gratitude Journal Prompts

Gratitude Journal

ONE
The Best Day of Your Life

" *The more you praise and celebrate your life, the more there is in life to celebrate.*"

— Oprah Winfrey

When you wake up each morning, there's no reason why this new day can't be the best day of your life. When we're grateful and appreciative of what we do have, we open ourselves up for unexpected surprises and new adventures.

Think back to a day in your life that you consider to be a great day. What happened that made your spirits soar? Who was with you? What emotions did you feel? Was any part of the day unexpected?

Don't stop there. Writing about your favorite day might trigger memories of other great days you've experienced. Write all about them.

There are even better days ahead. If you can create the best day of your life, what would happen? Who would you share the day with? What would you eat? Where would you be?

By writing this down and injecting it with positive energy, you'll set the motion to create it. This or something better can happen for you. The future holds limitless potential for more great days that you can't even begin to imagine in the present. In fact, every day contains miracles if you really stop to discover them.

TWO
All Smiles

" *A smile is a curve that sets everything straight.*"

— Phyllis Diller

Never underestimate the power of a smile. Whether from a stranger or someone you love, a smile directed your way brightens up the day. Whenever someone smiles, it's contagious; we can't help but smile back.

A smile is beautiful. It's a universal sign that you're open, friendly and giving. It connects us to one another. Studies have shown that just looking at photos of people smiling, especially the people you love, can have enormous mood-boosting effects. So if you're ever in a sour mood, smile! Even if it's for no reason. At first it may feel silly, but the right facial actions can stimulate feelings of joy.

We can immediately tell whether someone's smile is genuine or not on an instinctual level. There's a crinkling around the eyes, and an uplift of the cheeks and the corners of the mouth.

Children tend to smile 20x more per day than adults. That's because children are more in tune with the magic of the world and the pleasures in the little things that adults can take for granted.

Go ahead and try smiling more during the day. Smile at yourself in the mirror, look at smiling pictures of friends, try smiling at strangers. If you're shy, start small. Smile as you thank the cashier when s/he hands you your change and receipt, for example.

Note in your journal what you notice when you smile at people. Are they smiling back? Are they more open and inviting? What about the smiles that you've received today? List them and observe your own reactions to them.

Think about the lovely smiles of the people you know, or even the smiles of famous people. Whose smile makes you feel all gooey inside? What traits are reflected in their smiles?

Give yourself a genuine smile in the mirror. Note the beauty you radiate. What do you like about your own smile?

THREE
Teacher's Pet

" *It is the supreme art of the teacher to awaken joy in creative expression and knowledge.*"

— Albert Einstein

When the student is ready, the teacher appears, as the old adage goes. A teacher doesn't even have to be in the form of a person; we can learn from a cat, a flower, a single word.

Throughout your life, you've probably had various teachers in various forms, and you might have not even been aware of every one of them.

Begin by writing about a teacher whom inspired you and taught you something that changed your life for the better. It doesn't have to be a teacher in a conventional school setting. It could be a mentor in other areas of your life: a parent, a boss, a fitness trainer, a child, a famous figure in history you admire, etc.

Take the time to appreciate what they've done for you and how they've enriched your life. As you write about them, other inspiring teachers might come to mind.

Here are some ideas to start your entry:

Thank you, (teacher's name), for showing me that...

I admire you, (teacher's name), for....

From you, (teacher's name), I've learned how to...

FOUR
The Sixth Sense

" *Equipped with his five senses, man explores the universe around him and calls the adventure Science.*"

— Edwin Powell Hubble

What would you do without your five senses? Can you imagine not being able to see, hear, taste, touch or smell? It's something that we don't usually think about most of the time.

Some people are born without one or more of the five senses and they go on to do amazing things. Helen Keller, for example, was born deaf and blind. Instead of resigning to her fate, she had a burning desire to learn and to communicate with those around her, and she went on to become a brilliant student, author, lecturer and an inspiration to many.

Most of us are lucky enough to be able to listen to beautiful music or a lover's compliment, smell a fragrant flower or a cake baking in the oven, feel the warmth in a mother's hug or the softness of a blanket, taste a rain drop on our tongue or a delicious meal, and read books to further our education or this book to raise our gratitude.

Count your blessings. What are you thankful for in each of the five senses?

I love to see/look at/watch…

Hear/listen to…

Feel/touch…

Taste….

Smell…

What about a sixth sense? Are you good at empathizing with others? Do you have strong gut feelings? Are you in tune with animals? Write about these powerful gifts.

FIVE
The Bright Side

" *Knowing your own darkness is the best method for dealing with the darkness of other people.*"

— Carl Jung

The reason why so many people are addicted to being negative is that they receive energy from it. Yet it's an energy that ultimately drags us down. According to the Law of Attraction, we get what we send out into the universe, so it's always in our best interest to be sending out love, our highest vibration.

However, we can't be too hard on ourselves or on others when we're in a bad mood. It's unrealistic to be bubbly and happy all the time, and worse to reprimand yourself for not being this way. Nobody is this perfect. We just need to try and see the bright side of any situation. As long as we are doing that, we are growing.

Maybe you couldn't find your car keys, which made you late for work. Maybe your friend canceled on you at the last minute. Maybe your wife just informed you that she wants to get a divorce. It would be false to grin and bear it when life throws you a curve ball. Be honest with yourself. Feel the "negative" emotions for a moment; cry it out if you need to. There has to be an outlet for healthy emotional expression. You are experiencing it because it is there to teach you something, challenging you to take the high road.

Write about a time when you'd been proud of yourself for turning a negative situation into a positive one. When did you keep calm in the midst of chaos? Write about as many as you can think of. Add to the list as you experience them.

SIX
Our Other Mother

" *Think of all the beauty still left around you and be happy.*"

— Anne Frank

Mother nature is truly miraculous. From the grass beneath our feet to the beautiful sunset we are privileged to witness every evening, there's a world of miracles all around us. While her beauty is there for us to enjoy, whether we take the opportunity to or not, no one is immune to the benefits of nature. The water we drink, the air we breathe, the trees that give us shade and oxygen are just some of the ways that nature is essential to our livelihood.

When you're feeling sluggish after hours of working in a fluorescent-lit office, going outside, breathing in the fresh air and taking a brisk walk can do wonders for your vitality.

What do you appreciate about nature? It could be anything from the flowers that brighten your backyard to rock climbing on a mountain. Have you traveled somewhere that gives you peace? Is there a corner in the town where you live that you absolutely cherish? What have you noticed about nature on your way to work? What do you see above you, below you, all around you?

SEVEN:
Cinema Paradiso

" *A good film is when the price of the dinner, the theatre admission and the babysitter were worth it.*"

— Alfred Hitchcock

If you really think about it, film is really a form of hypnosis. When we're in a theatre, what we're experiencing is just hearing surround sound audio and watching a trick of the light. Yet, we're moved by it. Our hearts race, tears well up in our eyes, we fall in love with the characters, and we get swept up in the scenery, the action and the story.

Films can be entertaining and extremely profound. Great films inspire and shape us into better people.

What are some of your favorite films? What films did you love as a child? As a teen? As an adult? What did they teach you about love, about life? Did they inspire your fashion choices? Which scenes moved you the most? Made you laugh the hardest? Who's your favorite actor, your favorite character? What are some of your favorite lines? Why do you love these films so much?

EIGHT
Kids Say the Darndest Things

" *The pursuit of truth and beauty is a sphere of activity in which we are permitted to remain children all our lives.*"

— Lao Tzu

Children add such joy to our lives with their innocence, their bright outlooks and their endless curiosity. A child's laughter is infectious and they often say some clever things that would astound the wisest adult.

Are there any children in your life that bring you joy? They might be your own, the ones in your extended family, the kids in your neighborhood, in the local park. What can you learn from their exuberance? Do they keep you connected to your childish wonder?

Listen to them. What are some of the things they have said that amused you?

Get nostalgic about your own childhood for a moment. What's your favorite childhood memory? Who were you with? What season was it? What were you wearing? What were you doing? What did you feel?

NINE
Just Desserts

" *Work is the meat of life, pleasure the dessert.*"

— B.C. Forbes

Marcel Proust had his madeleines. Marie Antoinette had her cake and ate it too. What do you look forward to as a snack, or after a meal? Do cupcakes make you giddy? A warm apple strudel? Do you love anything chocolate? A French macaron? Gingerbread cookies?

Write about the desserts you love. Sometimes just looking at them sitting colorfully in a bakery window can bring joy.

Do you have a fond memory involving a dessert? Do you love to bake? Do you love a good hot chocolate at a café with a close friend? Do you love making chocolate chip cookies with your kids?

TEN
The Magic Mirror

" *Our hearts were drunk with a beauty our eyes could never see.*"

— George William Russell

" *Since love grows within you, so beauty grows. For love is the beauty of the soul.*"

— Saint Augustine

Due to media and societal pressures, it's common to have hang-ups about our bodies. In every culture, there's a standard of beauty to aspire to. Advertisements sell us products by highlighting our so-called flaws. We've grown accustomed to putting ourselves down whenever we look in the mirror. Maybe we've seen our parents do it, our friends do it, and even some of the most gorgeous celebrities do it in interviews. It's a bad habit we need to nip in the bud right now.

Look in the mirror. Don't judge, just observe. Look into your eyes, at the color, their warmness. Look at your skin, your hair, your body. Smile. If you can look at yourself in the mirror and not have one negative thing to say, you have surpassed 99% of the population. We can get there by stopping our self-sabotage.

Start by listing the things you *do* like about your appearance. Do you have nice eyes? A lovely smile? Slender hands? Do you like your belly button, your toes, your ears, the mole on your chin?

Start with a few. Focus on the positive and it will grow. Look into your eyes in the mirror and say "I'm beautiful" with conviction. How do you feel? Try repeating this exercise for the rest of the week. Has anything changed about the way you feel about yourself?

Continue to list what you like about yourself. Just by making the effort to do this you'll soon begin to see yourself as a beautiful, radiant being.

ELEVEN
Regarde le ciel

" *In the sky, there is no distinction of east and west; people create distinctions out of their own minds and then believe them to be true."*

— Buddha

" *Look at the sky. We are not alone. The whole universe is friendly to us and conspires only to give the best to those who dream and work."*

— Abdul Kalam

As a child, I used to look up, mesmerized to see dragons and pigs in the sky. As an adult, I'm still amazed by the beauty of a sky and often look up to admire the fluffy clouds, a clear blue sky, a plane leaving its track across it.

Sometimes all we have to do is look up to appreciate the day. Clouds can be such marvelous creations. Look up. What do you notice about the sky? Is it sunny? What color is it today? How does it affect your mood? Is the sky overcast? Does the layer of clouds make you feel as if there's a blanket of snow over your head? What can you make out from the shapes of clouds? Marshmallows? Animals? Faces? Mystical creatures?

TWELVE
A Night at the Museum

" *Living is like tearing through a museum. Not until later do you really start absorbing what you saw, thinking about it, looking it up in a book, and remembering—because you can't take it in all at once.*"

— Audrey Hepburn

Museums can be magnificent places for children, adolescents and adults alike. The majesty of stepping into a place and seeing ancient artifacts, treasured paintings and art pieces is profoundly nourishing for the soul.

One of my favorite museums is Anne Frank House in Amsterdam. To see the bedroom Anne lived in, the attic where she fell in love, and the real diaries she wrote in was one of the most touching experiences of my life.

What is your favorite museum? When did you go? How did you feel being inside it? What were the 5 best things that you saw or experienced in the museum?

What about museums that you would love to visit in the future?

THIRTEEN
Family Matters

"*It was on my fifth birthday that Papa put his hand on my shoulder and said, 'Remember, my son, if you ever need a helping hand, you'll find one at the end of your arm.'*"

— Sam Levenson

We choose our friends, but we don't choose our family. Sometimes we're lucky enough that our family members are also our friends. When there is friction in our relationships, we should still be appreciative that our family members are in our lives because they are all here for a reason.

Take each member of your immediate family and appreciate the positive things they have contributed to your life.

For example:

"I love you, Mom, for loving me unconditionally, even when I was hard to deal with as a teenager."

"I love you, Ben, for being a brother I can count on when I need someone to listen to."

If you didn't get along with a member of your family, dig deeper for the lesson. Maybe you didn't have one of your parents in your life and that makes you sad, or even angry. But it's possible to find the positive in everything.

How about:

"Thank you, Mom, for teaching me the value of having a mother. Thank you for teaching me to strive to be the best mom for my children."

Remember that everyone has their own stuff to deal with. Judgment or blame doesn't help anyone. Nobody is perfect and no family is perfect. While our family members may push our buttons and drive us crazy at times, they are here to help us, to challenge us, and thus shape us into our best selves, if we let ourselves learn the lessons.

You can continue giving thanks for the members of your extended family. Do you have a funny aunt, a cousin for a best friend, a doting grandmother? Or anybody else you can think of that has shaped you into the awesome person you are today?

Next, think about all the good times you've had with your family. What are your fondest memories?

Do you have any family rituals? Do you go on family vacations?

FOURTEEN
Bookworm

" *I cannot live without books.*"

— Thomas Jefferson

Studies show that people who read novels have an easier time emphasizing with others. Novels speak to our souls because they contain the truth of the soul. The relationship between the author and the reader is more intimate than any other form of art; the act of reading is an intimate one. Plus, what's better than cozying up with a good book and a blanket on a chilly night?

What books can you not live without? Who are your favorite authors? Your favorite fictional characters? What books have changed your life? Have you met a writer you've liked? Do you feel good just holding certain books? Are you in a book club? Favorite beginning in a book? Favorite ending? Best cover? Best lines in a book?

Gratitude Journal

FIFTEEN
A Tale of One City

" *I* have an affection for a great city. I feel safe in the neighborhood of man, and enjoy the sweet security of the streets."

— Henry Wadsworth Longfellow

When we live somewhere for a long time, our familiarity with our surroundings make us forget how great the place can be. The city or town that you are living in right now has some great advantages, doesn't it? See your city or town from a tourist's perspective:

What are some great places to visit? Are there friendly folks in town? Some good eats? Do you like the weather? The tranquility or the bustling excitement? The nature it has to offer, or the pretty architecture?

Big cities, or tiny towns, there's always something to appreciate. What are some things that are particular to your hometown that you love? What do you appreciate most?

SIXTEEN
The Shirt Off My Back

" *Clothes make the man. Naked people have little or no influence on society.*"

— Mark Twain

Whether you follow the trends, dress classically, or claim to have no style at all, clothes are a necessity in life. A well-tailored suit or dress can change the way you feel. You really do stand taller and act more confident in some clothes than others.

Look inside your closet. What are some of your favorite pieces and accessories? Where did you buy them? Do you associate certain pieces with a memorable experience? Did you fall in love while wearing a certain dress, for example? Did your mother give you your favorite tie? Did your child make you that bracelet that you cherish so much?

Fashion is an art form. Are there any designers or collections that you absolutely admire? What do you love about the brand or the creations? How do you feel in wearing their clothes?

SEVENTEEN
Your Gifts

" *God's gifts put the man's best dreams to shame.*"

— Elizabeth Barrett Browning

Don't be modest. You have a special talent or two. Perhaps more than a few. Everybody is good at something. You're here on earth to spread your gifts to others.

What are you good at? How has your kind words and positive actions affected others? Start by listing 3 things you are good at. Is it making someone laugh? Composing a song? Making a birdhouse? Keep adding to the list.

EIGHTEEN
Art Attack

" *No great artist ever sees things as they really are. If he did, he would cease to be an artist.*"

— Oscar Wilde

Art moves us in ways that we can't explain. Ever wonder what's behind Mona Lisa's enigmatic smile? The aliveness of Van Gogh's sunflowers? The passion in Rodin's The Kiss?

Art doesn't limit itself to paintings and sculptures; it's all around us. Maybe you've stumbled across a colorful mural on the side of a building, or your child gave you a charming drawing. I was once sitting on a subway train minding my own business when everybody around me started dancing as part of a flash mob performance. What a perk that was to my day!

What are some forms of art that you love? Do you have a favorite piece? Do you have a favorite artist? What is it about their sensibility and work that you love so much? Do you express yourself creatively in any way, such as with drawing, writing, dancing, playing music, knitting, etc.? Are there any exhibits or performances that you would love to see?

NINETEEN
A Season of Fate's Perfection

" *There are only two seasons—winter and Baseball."*

— Bill Veeck

The seasons change as we continue with the circle of life. Each one brings its own array of benefits and beauty.

Vivaldi loved the four seasons enough to compose violin concertos to express the full range of sensations in each of them. Which season do you prefer? What's great about spring or summer or autumn or winter? What do you love about the season you're in right now? Is it that you get to ski and make snowmen in the winter? Hang out at the beach in the summer? Watch the leaves turn gold and auburn in autumn? Smell the new flowers in bloom in the spring? Are there special events in your hometown that you look forward to each season?

TWENTY
Good to Great

" *Self-improvement is the name of the game, and your primary objective is to strengthen yourself, not to destroy an opponent.*"

— Maxwell Maltz

We tend to scold ourselves too much for not meeting our own, or other people's, expectations. It's easy to get trapped in the habit of putting ourselves down and not feeling good enough. There's a gravitational force with negativity that pulls us down, but if we make the effort to stay positive in our thinking, rising up will get easier and easier.

You have more gifts than you know. By making it a habit to focus on your positive traits, your self-esteem will grow, leading you to more opportunities and positive people.

Record all the reasons why you're proud of yourself. Did you grow up into a caring, responsible adult? Did you get a good education? Have a job you're good at? Have a great family? What about the things that you've done lately? Did you finish that birdhouse? Made some new friends? Got a new haircut or a raise? Baked a cake for a bake sale to raise money for the community? List as many things as you can think of, big or small.

TWENTY-ONE
Happy Meals

" *There is no sincerer love than the love of food."*

— George Bernard Shaw

They say that the fastest way to a man's heart is through his stomach. That's because feeding others is an act of love. On Thanksgiving, we give thanks for the food we eat and all the blessings in life. Food—eating it, making it, sharing it—is such an act of joy that it's no wonder there are entire TV channels dedicated to it.

Eating is both a necessity and a pleasure. Some people travel to the other side of the world just to get a bite of an authentic dish from a foreign country. I have a foodie friend who could spend hours on the phone just talking about the nuances of flavor and the ingredients detected in a meal.

What's your favorite dish? Do you love to cook for yourself or for others? Do you love to be fed by the people who love you? Do you love trying new restaurants and new chefs? Have you discovered a tasty dish on your travels? What would you like to learn to make? What good feelings do you associate with a particular dish?

TWENTY-TWO
Travel Bug

" *No one realizes how beautiful it is to travel until he comes home and rests his head on his old, familiar pillow.*"

— Lin Yutang

Whether it's across town or across the ocean, traveling is a great way to expand our perspectives and learn something different about other people, places and cultures. We inevitably come home a little changed, a little wiser.

Where have you traveled? Write about your positive experiences. What did you discover? Who did you share the experience with? What did you love about the food, the people, the architecture, the art? Did you make new friends? Did you have any unexpected adventures? Where have you been that you would love to return to? Do you have a travel bucket list?

TWENTY-THREE
All You Need is Love

"*Being deeply loved by someone gives you strength, while loving someone deeply gives you courage.*"

— Lao Tzu

Have you met the person you want to spend the rest of your life with? If so, who is s/he? What are the amazing qualities of this person? How does s/he make you feel?

If you haven't met your one yet, who do you love in your life? It could be a family member, a child, a pet, a friend, a celebrity. Make note of all the traits that you admire about them.

Loving someone takes courage, and so does receiving love. Cherish it because love is our driving force. When you have love in you, you are riding on the highest vibration in the universe.

Gratitude Journal

TWENTY-FOUR
The Adventures of...

" *One way to get the most out of life is to look upon it as an adventure.*"

— William Feather

Life is one great adventure made up of smaller adventures. It happens when we least expect it or when we're open to it.

What is the greatest adventure you've ever had? It could be anything from having a snowball fight when you were young to traveling to some exotic locale. Who was there? How old were you? What kind of adjectives would you use to describe the experience?

TWENTY-FIVE
I Feel Good

" *It takes more than just a good looking body. You've got to have the heart and soul to go with it.*"

— Epictetus

If you're like most people, you tend to take your health for granted until you're sick. That's when we realize what a gift it is to be in a healthy body where we can move without pain. Even when you are sick, it's still a blessing because it makes you appreciate your health even more.

What do you appreciate about your health?

Start with a list of ten. For example:

"Thank you for my healthy hands, which are holding this book."

"Thank you for my legs, which can take me from place to place easily."

"Thank you for my heart, which is pumping blood to the rest of my body, keeping me alive."

You can easily write more, a line for each part of your body and your organs, and all its amazing abilities.

TWENTY-SIX
God is My DJ

66 *The only thing better than singing is more singing.*"

— Ella Fitzgerald

Music is a great mood lifter and it raises our vibration. The voices from a choir can be absolutely angelic. Isn't it wonderful that a few notes can have infinite combinations? And there are always new musicians to discover and new songs coming out every day.

There's a man who sings and plays guitar on a street near where I live. He sings with his eyes closed and seems to be playing music just for the joy of it. I always smile when I pass by him because I can feel his sincere love for music.

Which bands/artists do you love? Do you have a good memory of attending a fabulous concert? Are there any upcoming concerts you would love to see? What do you admire about musicians? Do you sing, or play instruments yourself?

If you could, what instrument would you play or what style of music would you sing? Do you collect records, concert tees, ticket stubs, band parapher-nalia? Do you have a favorite song for different occasions? Do you pass by talented street musicians on your way to work? What song are you humming in your head right now?

TWENTY-SEVEN
Happy Birthday

" *God gave us the gift of life; it is up to us to give ourselves the gift of living well.*"

— Voltaire

When we were children, we were so excited about celebrating birthdays. Growing older, wiser and more self-reliant was a privilege, but as adults, many of us dread blowing out an additional candle each year. The truth is, the kids are right. Birthdays are something to celebrate. We know more now than we ever did because each year comes with a whole body of knowledge and insights we can only accumulate through experience.

What do you appreciate about growing older? What is your favorite birthday memory? What are some life lessons that you derived from your childhood, your teen years, your college years, your twenties, and so on?

TWENTY-EIGHT
Where the Heart Is

" *W here we love is home—home that our feet may leave, but not our hearts.*"

— Oliver Wendell Holmes

Our homes are not only safe shelters from the outside world, but private places for our hopes and dreams. We live in it, sleep in it, dream it in, cry in it, laugh in it, relax in it, fantasize in it, and play in it.

Can you imagine not having a roof over your head? Thankfully most of us do not even have to imagine that scenario. Whether you live in a tiny studio apartment, or a grand mansion, be thankful that you have a place to keep you warm from the outside cold, a place to call your own.

What do you love about your home? What about your childhood home? Do you have fond memories in any of the other homes you've had or visited? Perhaps a friend's or a close relative's home?

Is it full of positive energy, good people, and lovely decor? Do you have a favorite room or piece of furniture? Do you have a nice backyard where you can grow flowers and vegetables, or sit under a tree? Do you have kind neighbors? Why do the homes you love give you that warm, cozy feeling?

TWENTY-NINE
Best Gift Ever

" *A gift consists not in what is done or given, but in the intention of the giver or doer.*"

— Lucius Annaeus Seneca

Who doesn't love getting gifts?

What is the best gift you've ever received? It doesn't necessarily have to be a physical item. Who gave it to you? Why do you love it so much? How did you show appreciation?

Gratitude Journal

THIRTY
Role Models

" *E*veryone in society should be a role model, not only for their own self-respect, but for respect from others."

— Barry Bonds

There are countless great men and women in history and in our present day. They could be people you read about or people you know. Who better to help us reach greater heights than the people who has already gone there?

Who are your role models? It could be anyone from a historical figure, to your favorite entertainer, to Aunt Jo. What do you admire about them? What qualities do they have that make them great? What have they done to add value and joy to the world and to your life? What have you learned from them?

Gratitude Journal

THIRTY-ONE
Funny Face

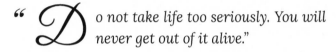"o not take life too seriously. You will never get out of it alive."

— Elbert Hubbard

Laughter really is the best medicine. It's the fastest way to lift yourself from a sour mood. Just turn on your favorite sitcom and try not to laugh.

What are some funny jokes or stories that you love? Do you have a funny friend whom you love to spend time with? Who are some funny comedians who never fail to crack you up? What are some funny TV shows, theatre pieces or movies that send you slapping your knees? Are you funny yourself? What have you said or done to make others laugh?

Gratitude Journal

THIRTY-TWO
Hope Floats

" *Take the first step in faith. You don't have to see the whole staircase, just take the first step.*"

— Martin Luther King, Jr

When your world turns dark, is there something that gives you hope? It could be a family member, hope for humanity, nature's brilliance, faith in God, friends to turn to, a pet's love—what lifts you out of darkness? Maybe it's just a nice hot bath, or turning on your favorite show, or drinking coffee with a friend. Make a list of them.

Gratitude Journal

THIRTY-THREE
A Little Help From Our Friends

" *A friend is one who knows you and loves you just the same.*"

— Elbert Hubbard

Studies have shown that our friends greatly contribute to our happiness, even more than our spouses and family members. We live longer when we have friends, the people who make up our network and community.

Who do you count as friends? Why are you so grateful that they are in your life? What are some good experiences that you've shared with them?

Here are some ideas to begin your entries:

"Thank you, Fred, for being in my life. You're such an inspiration because…"

"Susie is a great friend because she…"

Gratitude Journal

"I'm always happy to see Sam because…"

THIRTY-FOUR
The Art of Doing Nothing

" *The most luxurious thing to me is having an hour of my day, which rarely happens, to listen to my iPod and sit on my couch. That's how I unwind.*"

— Grant Achatz

In our fast-paced society, the art of doing nothing is something to be learned. We're always wired and it's becoming harder than ever to shut down our phones and computers to sit quietly and enjoy our own company.

What are your favorite ways to unwind? Is it sitting alone and meditating? Playing with your children? Baking? Doing a crossword puzzle? Nursing a warm cup of coffee? Lying on the couch? Swinging on a hammock and watching the sky?

THIRTY-FIVE
Please Give

" *The best way to cheer yourself up is to try to cheer somebody else up.*"

— Mark Twain

List 5 ways you gave others love today, or this week. It could be a kind word, a smile directed at a stranger, a present or a service.

Sometimes we are not aware of how much positivity we are impacting onto others with our positive actions until later on, or never at all. An open smile at a stranger, giving some pocket change to a homeless person, or the consideration of holding the door open for the person behind us can start a chain of positive reactions that inevitably comes back to us in other ways.

Be proud of all the ways you are contributing to a brighter world with your generosity.

Gratitude Journal

THIRTY-SIX
Please Take

" *Asking is the beginning of receiving. Make sure you don't go to the ocean with a teaspoon. At least take a bucket so the kids won't laugh at you.*"

— Jim Rohn

Allowing ourselves to receive can be a form of giving because we are allowing someone else to give and to feel good for doing so. As long we are not taking more than what's being offered or placing too much expectation on others, receiving can continue the flow of circuitry in relation to others.

What did you receive from friends, family or strangers that made you happy? Start with 5 things. Did a friend call out of the blue? Did you receive a nice letter in the mail? Did your child give you a piece of art they've created? Did your husband take you out to dinner? Did a neighbor give you a nice compliment? Gifts can come in a number of ways. Notice them and record them.

THIRTY-SEVEN
DIY

" *I* have the simplest tastes. I am always satisfied with the best."

— Oscar Wilde

The whole world is about creation. You wouldn't be here if you weren't created to begin with, and we are put on this earth to create: relationships, art, children, buildings, love…

There's nothing more satisfying than making something that's our own. What do you love to create? Do you love writing? Needlework? Carpentry? Music? Your own business?

Gratitude Journal

THIRTY-EIGHT
The Way You Move Me

" *T*he best and most beautiful things in the world cannot be seen or even touched—it must be felt with the heart."

— Helen Keller

What moves you? Is it a sad movie? A sweeping symphony? A lover whispering sweet nothings? The sight and sound of kids playing in the park? A sunset?

Sometimes a word from a friend, a line of poetry or something we read in the paper can have tremendous effect on our emotional states. What has touched your heart recently?

Gratitude Journal

THIRTY-NINE
Momento

" *T*hings are beautiful if you love them."

— Jean Anouilh

Appreciation for lovely, well-made things is perfectly healthy if we're being appreciative of the abundance that the world has to offer. Objects can have energy too, and we can get emotionally attached to them for various reasons.

Maybe a seashell collected from a lovely day at the beach gives you good feelings when you see it sitting on your windowsill. Or a jewelry box given from a loving grandmother makes you recollect the fond memories you've shared together. Or your husband gave you that necklace that you wear every day.

What treasured items do you hold near and dear to your heart and why?

Gratitude Journal

FORTY
The Transporter

" *E* very time I see an adult on a bicycle, I no longer despair for the future of the human race."

— H.G. Wells

Taking the subway or driving a car is so common that we don't even think about how inconvenient our lives would be without them. Walking to school or work might otherwise take us hours. Without an airplane, we wouldn't be able to travel to the other side of the world in under a day.

If you're ever stuck in traffic, make it a practice to be thankful for all the time that you have saved thanks to the invention of modern transportation. A bicycle in some parts of the world can make a huge difference for somebody, not to mention that feeling of liberation when you're cycling out in the open air.

What kind of transportation do you take? Which ones do you enjoy the most? Do you love roller-blading, sailing, pogo sticks, go-carts? How about Vespas and skateboards, limos and unicycles?

Do you like riding on a certain bus because it takes you along your hometown's finest attractions? Do you take care of your car like a family member?

FORTY-ONE
The Grand Palace

" *We shape our buildings; thereafter they shape us.*"

— Winston Churchill

Raise the roof (beams). Architects transform chaos into order in the form of beautiful buildings and houses. Whether it's a cozy home, a wonderful art museum or the ancient ruins, architecture can astound us by the way they transform a space to make us feel a certain way. The Taj Mahal was built to express the love of a man for a woman. Antoni Gaudi's buildings reflect his love of nature. Frank Gehry can scribble some strange shapes on paper and make it happen in reality.

What kind of architecture do you admire? Do you have a favorite architect? Have you ever been somewhere that took your breath away?

Gratitude Journal

FORTY-TWO
It's in the Photograph

" *A great photograph is one that fully expresses what one feels, in the deepest sense, about what is being photographed.*"

— Ansel Adams

Do you love leafing through old family photo albums? A photograph captures the soul, as they say. It can take you back to some cherished memories.

What photograph do you treasure? Who or what is in it and what does this person, place or thing mean to you?

Do you love taking photographs as well? Do you love art photography? Is there a photographer whom you admire?

Gratitude Journal

FORTY-THREE
Animal Farm

" *Animals are such agreeable friends—
they ask no questions; they pass no
criticisms.*"

— George Eliot

We tend to love animals so much that there are
countless films and stories about dogs and cats.
There are hospitals just for pets and entire stores
that sell pet accessories. I know a woman who spoils
her pet rabbits more than her sons.

Do you love animals? Do you have any pets? Do
you have a special bond with them? Do you enjoy
visiting the zoo? What kind of joy do animals bring
to you? What are some of your favorite stories
about animals?

Gratitude Journal

FORTY-FOUR
Home Run

" *People* ask me what I do in winter when there's no baseball. I'll tell you what I do. I stare out the window and wait for spring."

— Rogers Hornsby

Do you love playing sports, watching sports, or both? Do you have a jersey with your favorite athlete's name and number stitched on the back, or other sports paraphernalia? Do you look forward to certain seasons because of the sport you love?

What do you love about rooting for your favorite team? That feeling of pride when your hero scores a winning goal? How about the camaraderie between you and other fans? Or the fun of watching a live game and feeling the excitement all around you?

Which sports do you partake in? What do you love about it? Which sports would you love to learn how to play?

FORTY-FIVE
The Work

" *All labor that uplifts humanity has dignity and importance and should be undertaken with painstaking excellence.*"

— Martin Luther King, Jr.

What do you love about your job? Maybe you're lucky enough that you love what you do. Or maybe you're only working to pay the bills, but you're grateful that it provides you with the ability to pay the bills. Are there other reasons why you enjoy your job? Do you have a coworker that you consider as a friend? A boss that challenges you to do your best? The coffee in the staff lounge? The Christmas bonuses? That it's close to where you live?

Start with five things.

If you are currently unemployed, by staying grateful for whatever situation you are in, the positive energy will uplift you to the place where you want to be. Sure, you might be worried about money or your dignity, but what about the benefits of unemployment for the time being, such as having more time to spend with your kids? Or that you realize you have friends and family who are there for you in your time of distress? Or the time to figure out what you really want to do? Sometimes, people are dismissed from a job only to find their true passion.

FORTY-SIX
The Best Time of the Year

" *I once wanted to become an atheist, but I gave up—they have no holidays.*"

— Henry Youngman

What's your favorite holiday? Are there any holidays coming up that you are looking forward to? How do you plan to celebrate it? And with whom? What are some of your favorite holiday traditions? Songs? Memories?

FORTY-SEVEN
The Patriot

" *Patriotism is supporting your country all the time, and your government when it deserves it.*"

— Mark Twain

No country is perfect. In most countries, it's a national pastime to criticize the government. That only contributes to the negativity if we don't do something positive as a counteraction. In truth, we are responsible for our own happiness and that includes changing our perspective and focusing on the great things that our country have achieved. While we tend to complain to one another in our own country, it's harder to listen to members of other nations complain about us. Maybe you're more patriotic than you think.

There are great things to love about your country. What are they? The education system?

The language? The culture? The citizens? Certain traditions? Its literature and art? Certain laws you find fair? The delicious food?

FORTY-EIGHT
Flattery Will Get You
Everywhere

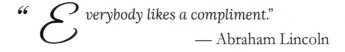 *"Everybody likes a compliment."*
— Abraham Lincoln

What are some nice things that people have complimented you on? List as many as you can remember.

What compliments have you given other people recently? List them as well. Everyone loves to be appreciated. Sometimes verbalizing appreciation can bring you closer to one another.

FORTY-NINE
Money In My Pocket

" *Money is to my social existence what health is to my body.*"

— Mason Cooley

Some of us have been taught to have a negative relationship with money. Contrary to popular belief, money is not the root of all evil. Its power is dependent on the people. We can do great things with money, and we can do some awful things; it's all in our choices.

Money is a necessity, like food and water. Without money, we don't have food, we don't have a home to live in, we can't buy the clothes to keep us warm, or the bus ticket to get us from place to place. Money allows us the means to travel and receive education. It helps our economy thrive and provide jobs to others.

Let go of lack mentality and begin appreciating the money that you do have. Every time you buy something, say thank you. What do you appreciate about having money in your life?

FIFTY
Straight Fs

" *If you're not failing every now and again, it's a sign you're not doing anything innovative.*"

— Woody Allen

Think of a problem or a hardship you've experienced in the past. While it might've been a difficult time in your life, what did it do to shape you into a better person?

Everyone fails at something. If we don't, we're not trying for anything. What have you failed at in life? Did failure teach you something useful? Did you do anything to overcome failure?

Now look at the great men and women who have failed, but went on to achieve great things. Which of their stories inspire you the most?

Gratitude Journal

FIFTY-ONE
Mere Mortals

" *The day which we fear as our last is but the birthday of our eternity.*"

— Lucius Annaeus Seneca

Our time here on earth is precious. Without sadness we wouldn't appreciate happiness, without sickness we wouldn't appreciate our health, and without death we would take life for granted.

Every day when you wake up in the morning, you are gifted with another day. What do you love about being alive?

If you've ever felt sad at losing a loved one, what did their passing teach you? Did it make you value your own life and the lives of those you love who are still with you? Did it inspire you to do more of the things you wanted to do?

Gratitude Journal

FIFTY-TWO
Never Stop Learning

" *I know that I am intelligent, because I know that I know nothing.*"

— Socrates

We really do learn something new every day. Attaining wisdom, and harnessing more love and gratitude is part of our soul's journey. Everyone is smart in different ways and there are different forms of intelligence, such as IQ and EQ (emotional intelligence). We tend to gravitate toward certain subjects depending on our desires.

What do you love learning? What do you appreciate about the education you've received? Do you have several degrees or learned profound lessons through the University of Life? Are you still in school or taking classes in what you're interested in?

What have you learned that has fascinated you? How do you continue to learn and evolve?

Gratitude Journal

MORE IDEAS

If you would like to improve a certain area of your life, such as in business or romance, you can devote a gratitude journal to it to inject more positive energy into that area.

For example, if you're having a hard time manifesting a relationship, you can write about all things love—the love you witness between other people, the love you give and receive with those around you, the romantic stories or films you love, what you love about yourself, what you would love in your own perfect partner. Doing so will raise your vibration into attracting the love you do want.

Giving gratitude doesn't have to stop at writing a journal. There are other creative ways of expressing thanks:

You can have a chalkboard in a prominent place like the kitchen or the living room where your family can add positive messages.

You can take photographs of the things or people that you love, print them out and post it on the fridge or anywhere you want where you can see them often. When you pass by them, you can say thank you and reflect on why you love them.

You can designate a jar where you, your family and friends can all put in messages. Set some pens and blank cards beside it with a note to urge your guests to write what they are thankful for. You can make a game out of reading each other's positive messages.

Or how about making something for your kids? For example, you can cut out the shape of a tree trunk from construction paper, tape it to the wall, and have the kids write what they are grateful for on paper leaves. Add leaves to the tree every day.

You can also create bulletin boards, vision boards, and find your own special way of surrounding yourself with more gratitude.

The point is to choose love every step of the way. Doing so will uplift your own mood and the energy of those around you.

Gratitude Journal

About the Author

Elizabeth N. Doyd is the author of the best-selling books *Write Him Off: Journal Prompts to Heal Your Broken Heart in 30 Days*, and *Gratitude Journal: 52 Writing Prompts to Celebrate Your Wonderful Life*. She also works as a relationship expert and spiritual counselor, having studied Kabbalah, Buddhism, hypnotherapy, astrology and Reiki.

Originally from Montana, Elizabeth has traveled around the world and currently lives in The Hague, Netherlands, with her husband, son and two Scottish terriers. Her highly practical self-help books are for those looking for guidance and healing in love, wealth and self-worth, and how to live each day with love, joy and purpose.

Gratitude Journal

Gratitude Journal